How
to Get to
Heaven

By GiGi Allen

G†G
Glory to God Publications
San Mateo, CA

Contents

How to Get to Heaven

God Loves You

*"For God so loved the world, that He gave His only begotten Son,
that whoever believes in Him shall not perish,
but have eternal life" -John 3:16*

*"Moreover, I will give you a new heart and put a new spirit within
you; and I will remove the heart of stone from your flesh
and give you a heart of flesh" -Ezekiel 36:26*

God loves you and He has a wonderful plan for your life. A plan
that will fulfill your heart's desires. A plan that will set you free
and bring you joy! He wants to have a relationship with you
and He wants you to be able to go to heaven, to live with Him
forever. But God gives everyone freedom of choice. You are free
to choose whether or not you want this relationship. God tells
us through His written Word, the Bible how to establish this
precious relationship.

"You must be born again" (John 3:7).

Why Do We Need to be Born Again?

God is the potter, we are the clay; He created us. But because of sin we are separated from God and we need to be born again/re-created in our spirit. We are eternal spirit beings that live inside a physical body. When we become born again we become a new creature with a new spirit. *"Therefore if anyone is in Christ, he is a new creature; the old things passed away, behold new things have come"* (2 Corinthians 5:17).

True heart contentment only comes from God through Jesus Christ. He created us for the purpose of fellowship. We can't have fellowship without relationship; we can't have a relationship without righteousness or right standing with God (sin free). We can receive this through Jesus Christ.

All have sinned and fallen short of the glory of God. All – no matter how good you have been you are still not perfect. Many people consider themselves to be good but being good is not enough to get you or me into heaven. Only Jesus lived a perfect life. Good works are not enough, it can't be earned! Only Jesus can bridge the gap for us to a Holy God.

Once I heard a newscaster say we are all God's children but that is not true. God originally created all of us but only those that are born again are in the family of God. Jesus said to some of the religious people of His day, *"You are of your father the devil..."* (John 8:44). Man must become born again to become God's child. In the Bible we see that the religious people of Jesus' day called the Pharisees were very focused on the external and appearance. Jesus pointed out that the Pharisees cleaned the outside of the cup but the inside was dead, unclean and full of self-indulgence (Matthew 23:27 NIV). He wanted them to focus on the inside, on the condition of their heart or spirit.

Born Again

The Bible says you must be born again. Jesus said "Do not be amazed that I said to you, 'You must be born again' (John 3:7).

"Jesus answered and said to him, "Truly, truly, I say to you, unless one is born again he cannot see the kingdom of God" (John 3:3).

"For I am not ashamed of the gospel, for it is the power of God for salvation to everyone who believes" (Rom. 1:16).

"Truly I say to you, unless you are converted and become like children, you will not enter the kingdom of heaven" (Matt. 18:3).

Now there was a man of the Pharisees, named Nicodemus, a ruler of the Jews; this man came to Jesus by night and said to Him, "Rabbi, we know that You have come from God as a teacher; for no one can do these signs that You do unless God is with him." Jesus answered and said to him, "Truly, truly, I say to you, unless one is born again he cannot see the kingdom of God."

Nicodemus said to Him, "How can a man be born when he is old? He cannot enter a second time into his mother's womb and be born, can he?" Jesus answered, "Truly, truly, I say to you, unless one is born of water and the Spirit he cannot enter into the kingdom of God. That which is born of the flesh is flesh, and that which is born of the Spirit is spirit. Do not be amazed that I said to you, 'You must be born again' ... (John 3:1-7).

"For God so loved the world, that He gave His only begotten Son, that whoever believes in Him shall not perish, but have eternal life. For God did not send the Son into the world to judge the world, but that the world might be saved through Him. (John 3:16-17).

Jesus is The Only Way

One time when I shared the gospel with a man, he said to me, " That seems so narrow that Jesus is the only way to heaven. What about all the other religions? " The Bible answers this for us; it says *"Enter through the narrow gate; for the gate is wide and the way is broad that leads to destruction, and there are many who enter through it. For the gate is small and the way is narrow that leads to life, and there are few who find it (Matthew 7:13,14).*

Yes, it is narrow. Yes, Jesus is the only way to heaven and to Father God. Jesus said, *"I am the way, and the truth, and the life; no one comes to the Father but through Me" (John 14:6).* Imagine if you gave up your only child to help someone, would you want your sacrifice to be rejected or to be in vain? God sent us help through Jesus Christ, His Son, He is the only way.

Salvation is a Free Gift

Salvation is a free gift through Jesus Christ. How can anyone argue with a free gift? God made it very easy for us. Even though the way is narrow it is available to ALL. It is not by works. It cannot be earned, but it is FREE. *"For by grace you have been saved through faith; and that not of yourselves, it is the gift of God; not as a result of works, so that no one may boast" (Ephesians 2:8-9).* It also says, *"For the wages of sin is death, but the free gift of God is eternal life in Christ Jesus our Lord" (Romans 6:23).* The wages of sin is death, refers to spiritual death which is separation from God. All sin leads to death and separates us from God, this is why we need Jesus. Through Jesus we can be born again made righteous and have eternal life.

How Do I Become Born Again?

It is simple, the Bible tells us how to do it. You pray to God, confess Jesus with your mouth and believe in your heart that God raised Him from the dead, in the Name of Jesus. Yes, it really is this simple, remember it is a gift!

A Prayer to Become Born Again

Dear God,
I come to you in the Name of Jesus.

Your Word says, *"... the one who comes to Me I will certainly not cast out" (John 6:37). So I know you won't cast me out, and I thank you for receiving me.*

You also said in your Word: *"If you confess with your mouth Jesus as Lord, and believe in your heart that God raised Him from the dead, you will be saved; for with the heart a person believes, resulting in righteousness, and with the mouth he confesses, resulting in salvation" (Romans 10:9-10).*

I believe in my heart that Jesus Christ is the Son of God. I believe He was raised from the dead, and I confess Him now as my Lord.
You also said *"Whoever will call on the Name of the Lord will be saved" (Romans 10:13).* I have called on the Name of the Lord Jesus and I receive salvation.

Thank you Lord, for my salvation!

Name_____   Date_____

Congratulations and welcome to the family of God.

A New Spirit- A New Creature

After praying that prayer the Bible says you are now in Christ and you are a new creature. *"Therefore if anyone is in Christ, he is a new creature; the old things passed away, behold new things have come" (2 Corinthians 5:17).* Your physical body remained the same but God gave you a new spirit, sometimes the Bible calls the spirit, the heart. It is not the physical heart, it is referring to the hidden man, the inner man. The following scripture helps us to understand this, *"but let it be the hidden person of the heart, with the imperishable quality of a gentle and quiet spirit, which is precious in the sight of God" (1 Peter 3:4).*

What is the new spirit like? The new spirit has been made in the image of Christ (Rom. 8:29). Love has been poured into your heart or new spirit. *"...the love of God has been poured out within our hearts through the Holy Spirit who was given to us" (Romans 5:5).* You have been changed on the inside.

The new spirit has wonderful characteristics. *"But the fruit of the Spirit is love, joy, peace, patience, kindness, goodness, faithfulness, gentleness, self-control...." (Galatians 5:22-23).*

Assurance of Salvation

And the testimony is this, that God has given us eternal life, and this life is in His Son. He who has the Son has the life; he who does not have the Son of God does not have the life. These things I have written to you who believe in the name of the Son of God, so that you may know that you have eternal life (1 John 5:11-13).

Joy

"For the joy of the Lord is your strength" (Neh. 8:10).

"A merry heart doeth good like a medicine..." (Proverbs 17:22).

There is such joy in becoming born again, such a sense of identity and purpose. God originally created us to have fellowship with Him. Without Him it is as though something is missing on the inside. But with Him there is inner contentment and joy. A sense of peace that all is well, we have found where we belong– in the family of God.

Once we become born again our real home our eternal home is in heaven.

"For our citizenship is in heaven..." (Phil. 3:20).

That is where we will go when our physical body dies. Our spirit does not die because of receiving Jesus Christ our spirit will go to heaven to live with God our Father forever.

"But you have come to Mount Zion and to the city of the living God, the heavenly Jerusalem, and to myriads of angels, to the general assembly and church of the first-born who are enrolled in heaven, and to God, the judge of all, and to the spirits of right-eous men made perfect" (Heb. 12:22-23).

"...rejoice that your names are recorded in heaven" (Luke 10:20).

Made Righteous

Righteousness is a gift, when you are born again Jesus takes your sin and gives you His righteousness. In this transference Jesus makes you able to stand before God washed clean of all sin, without guilt, shame, fear, inferiority or condemnation.

"He made Him who knew no sin to be sin on our behalf, so that we might become the righteousness of God in Him" (2 Corinthians 5:21).

"For if by the transgression of the one, death reigned through the one, much more those who receive the abundance of grace and of the GIFT OF RIGHTEOUSNESS will reign in life through the One, Jesus Christ" (Romans 5:17).

Again just like salvation this righteousness is not earned it is a gift. As we meditate on righteousness scriptures we will renew our minds so that we will see ourselves as made righteous instead of seeing ourselves as sinners. I am not saying that we are without sin, for all have sinned. But there has been a change in our spirit, in our core, in who we are, and in our identity. We are no longer to identify ourselves as old sinners stuck in sin. We have been set free by Christ. We are to see ourselves righteous— in right standing with God.

As we grow in our understanding of this change we will begin to live higher. As we believe it, we will walk in it. As we continue to receive the revelation of the gift of righteousness it will be made manifest in our lives.

"He justifies and accepts as righteous him who has (true) faith in Jesus" (Rom. 3:26 AMP).

" But by His doing you are in Christ Jesus, who became to us wisdom from God and righteousness and sanctification, and redemption..." (1 Cor. 1:30).

One With God

We are now one with God. He will never leave us or forsake us. Every where we go, He goes with us. We will never be alone. The life we now live, we live with Him , through Him and for Him! We are God carriers!

" But the one who joins himself to the Lord is one spirit with Him" (1 Corinthians 6:17).

"...For we are the temple of the living God; just as God said, "I WILL DWELL IN THEM AND WALK AMONG THEM; AND I WILL BE THEIR GOD, AND THEY SHALL BE MY PEOPLE" (2 Corinthians 6:16 NASB).

"You are from God, little children, and have overcome them; because greater is He who is in you than he who is in the world" (1 John 4:4 NASB).

Jesus said, "... I came that they may have life, and have it abundantly" (John 10:10 NASB).

"...for He Himself has said, "I WILL NEVER DESERT YOU, NOR WILL I EVER FORSAKE YOU," (Hebrews 13:5).

"I have been crucified with Christ; and it is no longer I who live, but Christ lives in me; and the life which I now live in the flesh I live by faith in the Son of God, who loved me and gave Himself up for me." (Gal. 2:20).

The Next Steps

Join a Church and Volunteer

The Word of God encourages us to attend church and gather together. It says, *"not forsaking our own assembling together, as is the habit of some, but encouraging one another..."* (Hebrews 10:25).

Volunteering helps with regular attendance and developing relationships within the church. This is your new family, your new brothers and sisters in Christ.

Your church family is where you will find support, encouragement, love and teaching. Your church family will be able to help you walk in this new life you have received through Jesus Christ.

As a family, we all contribute. *"Above all, keep fervent in your love for one another...As each one has received a special gift employ it in serving one another as good stewards of the manifold grace of God"* (1Peter 4:8, 10).

If you have not identified your gifts then simply start by volunteering in an area where there is a need, or ask one of the church leaders to help you identify an area that will be a good fit for you.

"... through love serve one another " (Galatians 5:13). "We know love by this, that He laid down His life for us; and we ought to lay down our lives for the brethren" (1John 3:16).

Attend a Bible Study

Many churches offer mid-week small group Bible studies. They are often designed for discussion, personal prayer requests and question and answer. You may have many questions and this is a great place to get them answered. Attending a small group Bible study needs to be emphasized. It is a great way to get plugged in and make relationships. It will help you grow as a Christian.

Forgiveness

At the new birth we were set free from sin, it cannot have dominion over us any longer. At the new birth we also received forgiveness for all of our past sins. However from that point forward sin must be dealt with individually. Each sin should be repented for; sin is unrighteousness and it is not pleasing to God. It is like a clog in a pipe, it blocks the flow. Lack of forgiveness blocks the flow spiritually in our relationship with God.

First John 1:9 says, *"If we confess our sins, He is faithful and righteous to forgive us our sins and to cleanse us from all unrighteousness."* That is a good scripture to memorize, as well as *"...the blood of Jesus His Son cleanses us from all sin" (1 John 1:7).* However this is not automatic each sin needs to be taken before God and be repented for. True repentance is not just having remorse and saying sorry. It is also turning from the sin, committing to change, to try to stay sin free.

How does God forgive? Completely! He remembers it no more. *"...for I will forgive their iniquity, and their sin I will remember no more" (Jeremiah 31:34). " FOR I WLL BE MERCIFUL TO THEIR INIQUITIES, AND I WILL REMEMBER THEIR SINS NO MORE" (Hebrews 8:12). "AND THEIR SINS AND THEIR LAWLESS DEEDS I WILL REMEMBER NO MORE"(Hebrews 10:17).*

God's forgiveness allows us to live free from condemnation. *"Therefore there is now no condemnation for those who are in Christ Jesus" (Romans 8:1).* Since He chooses not to remember our sin then we are not to dwell on it either. This Scripture is a good encouragement for us and shows us where our focus should be *"...but one thing I do: forgetting what lies behind and reaching forward to what lies ahead, I press on toward the goal for the prize of the upward call of God in Christ Jesus (Philippians 3:13-14 NASB).*

Read The Bible

It is important to read the Bible every day. A good place to start is in the New Testament in the book of John. Reading the Bible will help you to get to know God better and it will teach you His will. It will help you to renew your mind, to understand God's thoughts and to be successful.

"This book of the law shall not depart from your mouth, but you shall meditate on it day and night, so that you may be careful to do according to all that is written in it; for then you will make your way prosperous, and then you will have success" (Joshua 1:8).

We renew our mind by reading the Word of God. *"And do not be conformed to this world, but be transformed by the renewing of your mind, so that you may prove what the will of God is, that which is good and acceptable and perfect" (Romans 12:2).*

"Do your best to present yourself to God as one approved, a worker who does not need to be ashamed and who correctly handles the word of truth" (2 Timothy 2:15 NIV)

The Bible won't do any good if it just sits on your night stand, you must read it and get it into your mind and heart. There are several good translations such as New International Version (NIV), New American Standard Bible (NASB), and New King James (NKJ). You can purchase one from a Christian bookstore, Amazon.com or download one onto an iPad or iPhone. Some churches give them away for free when you are just getting started, it's worth asking about.

The Heart and The Word

When Jesus was on earth he told the disciples the meaning of a parable. Those with a good heart will receive the word of God, hold on to it and bear fruit. Let's look at His words in Luke 8:5-15.

"The sower went out to sow his seed; and as he sowed, some fell beside the road, and it was trampled under foot and the birds of the air ate it up. Other *seed* fell on rocky *soil*, and as soon as it grew up, it withered away, because it had no moisture. Other *seed* fell among the thorns; and the thorns grew up with it and choked it out. Other *seed* fell into the good soil, and grew up, and produced a crop a hundred times as great." As He said these things, He would call out, "He who has ears to hear, let him hear."

His disciples *began* questioning Him as to what this parable meant. And He said, "To you it has been granted to know the mysteries of the kingdom of God, but to the rest *it is* in parables, so that SEEING THEY MAY NOT SEE, AND HEARING THEY MAY NOT UNDERSTAND.
"Now the parable is this: the seed is the word of God. Those beside the road are those who have heard; then the devil comes and takes away the word from their heart, so that they will not believe and be saved. Those on the rocky *soil are* those who, when they hear, receive the word with joy; and these have no *firm* root; they believe for a while, and in time of temptation fall away.

The *seed* which fell among the thorns, these are the ones who have heard, and as they go on their way they are choked with worries and riches and pleasures of *this* life, and bring no fruit to maturity. But the *seed* in the good soil, these are the ones who have heard the word in an honest and good heart, and hold it fast, and bear fruit with perseverance. "

Guard your heart, and value God's Word, so you will be fruitful.

The Word of God

The following scriptures teach us the value of the Word of God:

"All Scripture is inspired by God and profitable for teaching, for reproof, for correction, for training in righteousness; so that the man of God may be adequate, equipped for every good work" (2 Timothy 3:16-17 NASB).
"BUT THE WORD OF THE LORD ENDURES FOREVER" (1 Peter 1:25 NASB).

"But He answered and said, "It is written, 'MAN SHALL NOT LIVE ON BREAD ALONE, BUT ON EVERY WORD THAT PROCEEDS OUT OF THE MOUTH OF GOD'" (Matthew 4:4 NASB).

"...like newborn babies, long for the pure milk of the word, so that by it you may grow in respect to salvation,..." (1 Peter 2:2 NASB).

"The law of the LORD is perfect, restoring the soul; The testimony of the LORD is sure, making wise the simple. The precepts of the LORD are right, rejoicing the heart; The commandment of the LORD is pure, enlightening the eyes" (Psalm 19:7-8 NASB).

"Your word is a lamp to my feet And a light to my path" (Psalm 119:105 NASB).

"For the word of God is living and active and sharper than any two-edged sword, and piercing as far as the division of soul and spirit, of both joints and marrow, and able to judge the thoughts and intentions of the heart" (Hebrews 4:12 NASB).

"So Jesus was saying to those Jews who had believed Him, "If you continue in My word, then you are truly disciples of Mine; and you will know the truth, and the truth will make you free" (John 8:31-32 NASB).

Pray

As well as reading the Bible prayer also strengthens your relationship with God. We pray to God our Father in the name of Jesus. Because of Jesus we have access to God. Jesus said, *" Until now you have asked for nothing in My name; ask and you will receive, so that your joy may be made full" (John 16:24).* We can turn all of our concerns over to God in prayer, so that we can stay in peace.

"Be anxious for nothing, but in everything by prayer and supplication with thanksgiving let your requests be made known to God. And the peace of God, which surpasses all comprehension, will guard your hearts and your minds in Christ Jesus" (Phil.4:6-7). He cares about us, He hears us and He is faithful to answer. God wants us to include Him in our lives through prayer.

"Rejoice always; pray without ceasing; in everything give thanks; for this is God's will for you in Christ Jesus" (1Thes. 5:16-18).

He who did not spare His own Son, but delivered Him over for us all, how will He not also with Him freely give us all things? (Romans 8:32)

God knows what we have need of before we ask yet He still tells us to ask (as seen in Matthew 6:8-9).

John Wesley said, "It seems God is limited by our prayer life- that He can do nothing for humanity unless someone asks Him." The Bible also supports this statement, it says *"You do not have because you do not ask" (James 4:2).* This understanding should motivate us to pray.

Water Baptism

Ask to be water baptized; baptism is a command in scripture. Baptism means to "dip; immersion or submersion" as a symbol of purification and sanctification. Baptism is for born again believers. It is an outward sign of an inward change. *"Go therefore and make disciples of all the nations, baptizing them in the name of the Father and the Son and the Holy Spirit" (Matthew 28:19).*

Even Jesus Himself was baptized. This public acknowledgement helps to solidify our decision and it is a witness to others of our change and dedication to Christ. It is an opportunity to invite others to celebrate the new life we have received, and to share the good news gospel of Jesus Christ with them.

"Therefore we have been buried with Him through baptism into death, in order that as Christ was raised from the dead through the glory of the Father, so we too might walk in newness of life. For we have become united with Him in the likeness of His death, certainly we shall be also in the likeness of His resurrection" (Rom. 6:4-5).

"...and this water symbolizes baptism that now saves you also— not the removal of dirt from the body but the pledge of a clear conscience toward God. It saves you by the resurrection of Jesus Christ," (1 Peter 3:21 NIV).

"...having been buried with Him in baptism, in which you were also raised up with Him through faith in the working of God, who raised Him from the dead" (Col.2:12).

Baptism in the Holy Spirit

"I will ask the Father, and He will give you another Helper, that He may be with you forever; that is the Spirit of truth, whom the world cannot receive, because it does not see Him or know Him, but you know Him because He abides with you and will be in you (John 14:16,17).

According to Scripture there is a difference between being born of the Spirit and being filled with the Spirit. Those born of the Spirit (born again) have eternal life and have been made a "new creature" (as seen in 2 Corinthians 5:17). Only those born again can be filled with the Holy Spirit—our helper. The following information and steps are intended to help you receive the Holy Spirit:

1. God gave the Holy Spirit on the day of Pentecost.

2. Anyone that is saved/ born again is ready to receive the baptism of the Holy Spirit.

3. Ask. *"You do not have because you do not ask"* (James 4:2).

4. Believe you will receive what you ask for.

"Now suppose one of you fathers is asked by his son for a fish; he will not give him a snake instead of a fish, will he? Or if he is asked for an egg, he will not give him a scorpion, will he? If you then, being evil, know how to give good gifts to your children, how much more will your heavenly Father give the Holy Spirit to those who ask Him?" (Luke 11:11-13).

Peter said to them, *"Repent, and each of you be baptized in the name of Jesus Christ for the forgiveness of your sins; and you will receive the gift of the Holy Spirit. For the promise is for you..."* (Acts 2 :38,39).

Baptism in the Holy Spirit

5. God leads He does not force.

"For all who are being led by the Spirit of God, these are sons of God" (Rom. 8:14). God gives the gift but the individual does the speaking. *"And they were all filled with the Holy Spirit and began to speak with other tongues, as the Spirit was giving them utterance"* (Acts 2:4).

"But you, beloved, building yourselves up on your most holy faith, praying in the Holy Spirit" (Jude 1:20). The Apostle Paul said, *"I thank God I speak in tongues more than you all"* (1 Cor. 14:18).

"He who believes in Me, as the Scripture said, 'From his innermost being will flow rivers of living water.' But this He spoke of the Spirit, whom those who believed in Him were to receive..." (John 7:38,39). *"For they were hearing them speaking with tongues and exalting God"* (Acts 10:46).

6. Expect to receive when hands are laid on you.

"And Philip went down to the city of Samaria and began proclaiming Christ to them. But when they believed Philip preaching the good news about the kingdom of God and the name of Jesus Christ, they were being baptized, men and women alike. Now when the apostles in Jerusalem heard that Samaria had received the word of God, they sent them Peter and John, who came down and prayed for them that they might receive the Holy Spirit.

For He had not yet fallen upon any of them; they had simply been baptized in the name of the Lord Jesus.

Then they began laying their hands on them, and they were receiving the Holy Spirit" (Acts 8:5,12,14-17).

Trust God

God is worthy of our trust, we can lean on Him; He is faithful.

"Trust in the Lord with all your heart, and do not lean on your own understanding. In all your ways acknowledge Him, and He will make your paths straight" (Proverbs 3:5-6).

"God is faithful..." (1 Cor. 1:9).

"...I WILL PUT MY TRUST IN HIM..." (Heb. 2: 13).

Congratulations on becoming born again and welcome to the family of God. You have been forgiven and set free from the dominion of sin. There is no condemnation for those that are in Christ Jesus. You have been made righteous by Jesus Christ, therefore you are in right standing with God. Remember to apply the following:

1. If you sin again, repent and receive forgiveness

2. Pray

3. Read the Bible

4. Join a church

5. Volunteer at church

6. Attend a Bible study

7. Ask to be water baptized

8. Receive the baptism in the Holy Spirit

9. Trust God

10. Continue your Christian education
    Victory International Church has a free Bible School on line. You can listen to classes by going to our website www.victoryic.org then go to the Victory Bible School page. We hope this will be a blessing to you.

Books by GiGi Allen

Walking With God (a study guide)

The Creative Power of Your Words

Bible Highlights

How to Get to Heaven

For Children:

Scriptures to Color (volume 1-7) This is a reproducible Scripture memory coloring book for children. It is also available in Spanish.

Ucan The Toucan

How to Draw (Cartoons for Beginners)

My First Animal Coloring Book

My Alphabet Coloring Book

49872778R00016

Made in the USA
Charleston, SC
09 December 2015